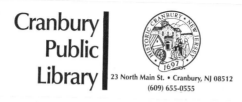

What Can Dig?

Patricia Whitehouse

Heinemann Library
Chicago, Illinois

Customer Service 888-454-2279
Visit our website at www.heinemannlibrary.com

Designed by Sue Emerson, Heinemann Library; Page layout by Que-Net Media™
Printed and bound in the U.S.A. by Lake Book Manufacturing
Photo research by Bill Broyles

08 07 06 05 04
10 9 8 7 6 5 4 3 2 1

Library of Congress Cataloging-in-Publication Data
Whitehouse, Patricia, 1958-
   What can dig? / Patricia Whitehouse.
      p. cm. – (What can?)
Includes index.
   ISBN 1-4034-4369-6 (HC), 1-4034-4376-9 (Pbk.)
   1. Excavating machinery–Juvenile literature. [1. Excavation. 2. Tunneling. 3. Excavating machinery. 4. Animals–Habits and behavior.] I. Title.
   TA732.W48 2003
   624.1'52–dc21

                              2003001010

Acknowledgments
The author and publishers are grateful to the following for permission to reproduce copyright material:
p. 4 Creatas; pp. 5, 18 Stephen J. Krasemann/DRK Photo; p. 6 Adam Jones/Visuals Unlimited; p. 7 Joe McDonald/Corbis; p. 8 Kevin Schafer/Corbis; p. 9 John Sohlden/Visuals Unlimited; p. 10 Amy Wiley/Wales/Index Stock Imagery; p. 11 John Winnie, Jr./DRK Photo; pp. 12, 17 Jeff Foott/DRK Photo; p. 13 Mark Newman/Visuals Unlimited; p. 14 Dwight Kuhn; p. 15 Anthony Bannister/Gallo Images/Corbis; p. 16 Ken Lucas/Visuals Unlimited; p. 19 Science VU/FNL/Visuals Unlimited; p. 20 P. Hershkowitz/Bruce Coleman Inc.; p. 21 Peter Christopher/Masterfile; p. 22 (row 1, L-R) Kevin R. Morris/Corbis, Mark Newman/Visuals Unlimited; (row 2, L-R) Corbis, Ken Lucas/Visuals Unlimited; p. 23 (row 1, L-R) Stephen J. Krasemann/DRK Photo, Joe McDonald/Corbis, Dwight Kuhn; (row 2, L-R) Peter Christopher/Masterfile, Anthony Bannister/Gallo Images/Corbis, Larry Lipsky/DRK Photo; (row 3, L-R) Jeff Foott/DRK Photo, Science VU/FNL/Visuals Unlimited; p. 24 (row 1, L-R) Mark Newman/Visuals Unlimited, Corbis, Ken Lucas/Visuals Unlimited; (row 2) Kevin R. Morris/Corbis; back cover (L-R) John Sohlden/Visuals Unlimited, Stephen J. Krasemann/DRK Photo

Cover photograph by Kevin Schafer/Corbis

Every effort has been made to contact copyright holders of any material reproduced in this book. Any omissions will be rectified in subsequent printings if notice is given to the publisher.

Special thanks to our advisory panel for their help in the preparation of this book:
Alice Bethke, Library Consultant
Palo Alto, CA

Eileen Day, Preschool Teacher
Chicago, IL

Kathleen Gilbert,
Second Grade Teacher
Round Rock, TX

Sandra Gilbert,
Library Media Specialist
Fiest Elementary School
Houston, TX

Jan Gobeille,
Kindergarten Teacher
Garfield Elementary
Oakland, CA

Angela Leeper,
Educational Consultant
Wake Forest, NC

Some words are shown in bold, **like this.**
You can find them in the picture glossary on page 23.

Contents

What Is Digging?

Digging is making a hole.

Some living things dig holes to make hiding places.

Other things dig to make homes or **nests.**

How Do Living Things Dig?

Some living things dig by using tools.

This chimpanzee is digging for ants with a stick.

Other living things use parts of their bodies to dig.

This **kangaroo rat** is digging with its paws.

Can Small Animals Dig?

Some small animals dig.

Foxes dig with their paws to find food.

Moles are small animals that dig.

They use their big front feet to dig holes in the ground.

Can Big Animals Dig?

Dogs are big animals that dig.

They dig to hide food.

Bears are big animals that dig.

They dig to find **roots** to eat.

Can Fish Dig?

Some fish can dig.

A **grunion** twists its body into the sand to dig.

Some salmon can dig.

They use their tails to dig a **nest** for their eggs.

Can Things Dig with Their Mouths?

Worms dig with their mouths.

They eat dirt as they crawl through it.

mandibles

Ants dig with special parts of their mouths.

The parts are called **mandibles.**

Can Things Dig with Their Feet?

foot

Clams have a foot.

They use it to dig into the muddy ocean floor.

Desert tortoises dig with their front feet.

They dig holes called burrows so they can stay cool.

Can Machines Dig?

A **backhoe** is a machine that digs.

It scoops dirt from the ground.

This **tunnel boring machine** digs under ground.

It makes underground **tunnels** for cars.

Can People Dig?

People can dig with their hands.

These children are digging in
the sand.

People can use machines to help them dig.

This man is using a machine to dig **coal**.

Quiz

Which of these things can dig?

Can you find them in the book?

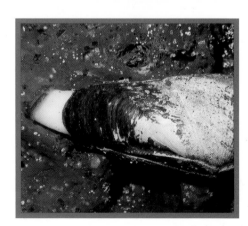

Picture Glossary

backhoe
page 18

kangaroo rat
page 7

roots
page 11

coal
page 21

mandibles
(MAN-di-buhls)
page 15

tunnel
page 19

grunion
(GRUN-yun)
page 12

nest
pages 5, 13

tunnel boring machine
page 19

Note to Parents and Teachers

Reading for information is an important part of a child's literacy development. Learning begins with a question about something. Help children think of themselves as investigators and researchers by encouraging their questions about the world around them. Each chapter in this book begins with a question that helps categorize the types of things that dig. Read each question together. Look at the pictures. Can children think of other digging things in each category? Discuss where you might find the answers. Assist children in using the picture glossary and the index to practice new vocabulary and research skills.

Index

Answers to quiz on page 22

Salmon, people, and clams can dig.

Some machines can dig, but they need people to make them work.